You're My Cup of Tea

Special Moments, Special Friends

Written and compiled by Virginia Reynolds

Illustrated by Maret Hensick

PETER PAUPER PRESS, INC.

WHITE PLAINS, NEW YORK

For Jo, my pink tea friend,
and the other decaffeinated writers

Designed by Heather Zschock

The Tea Party, by Josephine Hausam,
is used by permission.

Illustrations copyright © 2000
Maret Hensick, licensed by Schurman Design

Text copyright © 2000
Peter Pauper Press, Inc.
202 Mamaroneck Avenue
White Plains, NY 10601
All rights reserved
ISBN 0-88088-396-0
Printed in China
7 6 5 4 3 2 1

You're My
Cup of Tea

Special Moments, Special Friends

Introduction

What is it about tea and friends that goes so well together? Maybe it's the companionship of secrets shared over a steaming pot of tea. Or, maybe it brings back recollections of childhood tea parties savored in the sunshine. Whatever the reason, you don't need an excuse to relax with a friend for a while, treasuring old memories, or creating new ones. The kettle's whistling . . . sip and enjoy.

V. R.

The Tea Party

You graciously come to be with me.
We play a grown-up tea party.

I set out two cups—carefully.
One for you, one for me.

We sit at the table, knee to knee.
I pour the tea. You smile at me.

Lifting cups to our lips,
We sip—delicately.

You offer cake. I take a bite.
It tastes just right.

Just you and me.

• Josephine Hausam •

I guess you could say that you suit me . . . to a "T!"

Each friendship is a "custom blend," with a character all its own.

Like teacups,
friends come in all shapes
and sizes, and every one
is rare and precious.

The glow of
friendship, like
a fine pot of tea,
warms us inside
and out.

The laughter of
friends sounds like
tinkling silver on
fine porcelain.

A hot cup of tea
and a good friend
can do wonders
for your sanity.

Tea parties bring out
the best in both host
and guest.

When we get together,
there's always lots of
frivoli-"tea."

There are friends and teas
to suit every mood.

A good friend will stick
by you long after the
teacups are cold.

There are so many
possibili-"teas" for fun
and laughter when
we're together!

Careful measuring
will produce a perfect cup
of tea, but true friends
don't need to measure
their words.

Sometimes you
need your friends
and your tea with
lemon; sometimes
you want them
with sugar and
cream.

Love and scandal
are the best
sweeteners of tea.

• Henry Fielding •

Our friendship
is brewed with
companionship,
lots of laughter,
and a little spice!

I can pour my
heart out to you
while you pour
out the tea.

Friendship can be light
and refreshing, like iced
tea on a summer day.
Or, friendship can be rich
and hearty, like a stout
cup of English tea.

"Take some more tea,"
the March Hare said to
Alice very earnestly.

• Lewis Carroll •

Our conversation flows, full of lively splashes, like tea from the teapot.

I love spending
quali-"tea" time
with you!

Over tea, we share
our secrets—and our
love of delicious
tea-time goodies.

Let your troubles float
away on the steam from the
teapot as you unburden
your soul to a friend.

When life gets too busy,
slow down, and invite a
friend to tea.

Our get-togethers
are always
so zes-"tea."

A cup of tea will
quench your thirst,
while a good friend will
satisfy your thirst
for conversation.

The delicate aroma
of tea brings back so
many happy memories
of the times we've
spent together.

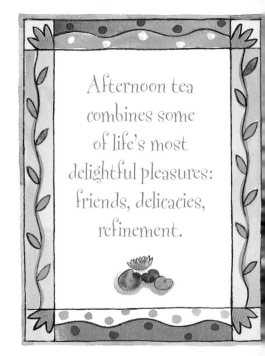

Afternoon tea combines some of life's most delightful pleasures: friends, delicacies, refinement.

We don't even
need to talk . . .
just share the silent
dialogue of pouring,
stirring, sipping.

If I had all the
tea in China,
I couldn't
buy a better
friend than you!

A perfect
memory for me:
a plate of sweets,
a pot of tea—
and thee!

The clear colors of freshly brewed tea— ruby red, gold, delicate green—reflect the ever-changing aspects of friendship.

Our friendship is
the tea cozy that keeps
our shared secrets
safe and warm.

We have so much in common, but we always respect each other's individuali-"tea."

When we're
together, the
simplicity of sharing
a humble cup of tea
seems elegant
and grand!

A good friend
can read you as a
fortune teller reads
her tea leaves.

You provide exactly
the right blend of tea
and sympathy!

When I'm worried, you lead me to a place of peace and tranquili-"tea."

We cherish each other despite our little imperfections, the way we would cherish an antique tea service with a few tiny cracks.

Come along inside . . .
We'll see if tea and buns
can make the world
a better place.

• Kenneth Grahame, *The Wind In The Willows* •

A cup of tea and
a visit from a friend
are welcome any
time of day.

We go together
like tea and
scones, cups
and saucers.

When we have
tea together, we
can behave like
giggly little girls.

Choose your
friends as carefully
as you would the
finest tea leaves.

Taking tea with
a friend is really a
way of pampering
yourself.

When the kettle whistles, I think of tea–and when I think of tea, I think of sharing it with you.

Having a tea party with friends sparks my creativi-"tea."

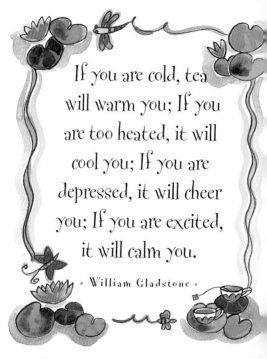

If you are cold, tea will warm you; If you are too heated, it will cool you; If you are depressed, it will cheer you; If you are excited, it will calm you.

• William Gladstone •

(Of course, Mr. Gladstone's remarks are true, but they are just as true of friends as they are of tea!)

Tea from a paper cup
would taste like nectar
if served by the loving
hands of a friend.

There's no pretense
between good friends—
our words are full of
sinceri-"tea."

The simplest
of pleasures can
nourish the most
complex of
relationships.

When life hands
you lemons,
friends brew tea.

Friends can give
us our lumps when
we deserve them,
but tactfully.

Whether it's a
few minutes or a
few hours, tea with
friends is an oasis
of peace in a busy
world.

With tea and with friends, the quality of the ingredients is important.

Dear friend, as long
as we're together,
our hearts and
teacups will never
be emp-"tea."

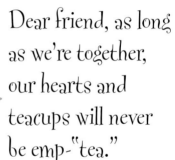

Tea is drunk to forget the din of the world.

• T'ien Yiheng •

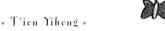

Tea is at its best
when garnished with
crisp conversation.

You can be on your best behavior when serving tea to friends, and they won't mind a bit.

We can pour
our souls out
into teacups, and
drink to each
other.

How many times
have we solved the
world's problems
over a cup of tea?

In the teacups,
I see two reflections—
yours and mine.
How alike we are!

It's so much easier to
talk about things when
you can wash them down
with a cup of tea.

I guess you could say
that spending time with
friends is my favorite
activi-"tea."

Shall we nibble on some scrumptious gossip?